Easy Braids, Barrettes and Bows

Written by Judy Ann Sadler

Illustrated by Sarah Jane English

KIDS CAN PRESS

To my beautiful sisters, Mary, Linda, Pauline and Irene
— our lives are braided together with love.

Special thanks to Kathy Machesney, Sandra Vanier and
Audrey Allen for their time and expertise.

Text copyright © 1997 by Judy Ann Sadler
Illustrations copyright © 1997 by Sarah Jane English
Photographs copyright © 1997 by Ray Boudreau

KIDS CAN DO IT and the 🖊 logo are trade marks of Kids Can Press Ltd.

Published in Canada by
Kids Can Press Ltd.
29 Birch Avenue
Toronto, ON M4V 1E2

Published in the U.S. by
Kids Can Press Ltd.
85 River Rock Drive, Suite 202
Buffalo, NY 14207

Edited by Laurie Wark
Designed by Karen Powers and Marie Bartholomew

Printed in Hong Kong by Wing King Tong Company Limited

CMC 97 0 9 8 7 6 5 4 3

Canadian Cataloguing in Publication Data
Sadler, Judy Ann, 1959 – .
Easy braids, barrettes and bows

(Kids can do it)
ISBN 1-55074-325-2

1. Hairstyles — Juvenile literature. 2. Braids (Hairdressing) — Juvenile literature.
3. Hair-work — Juvenile literature. 4. Handicraft — Juvenile literature.
I. English, Sarah Jane, 1956– . II. Title. III. Series.

TT975.S22 1996   j646.7'245   C96-931607-0

Kids Can Press is a Nelvana company

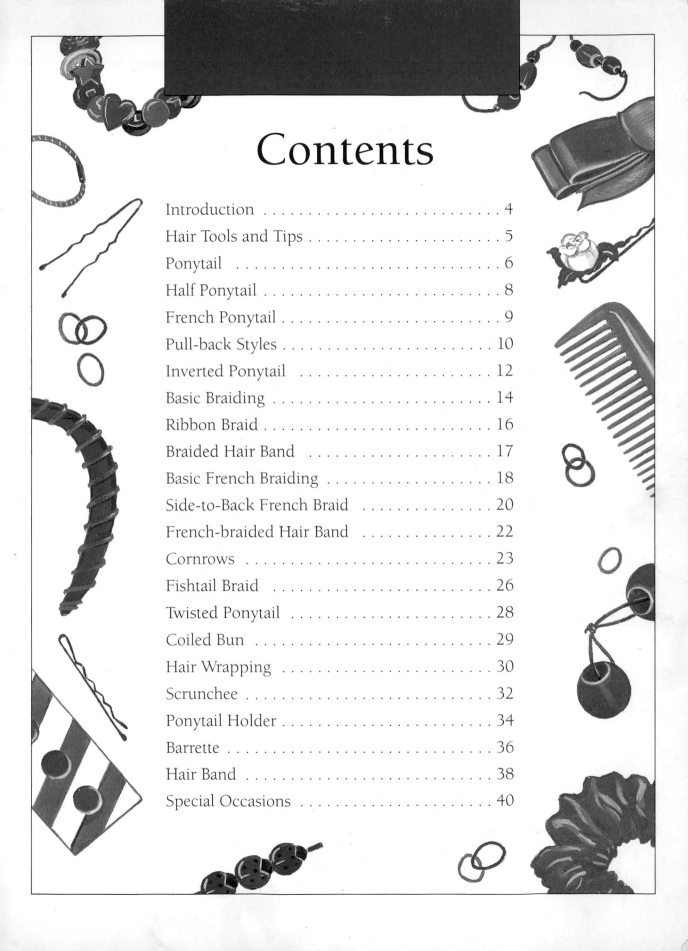

Contents

Introduction

Would you believe that over the centuries people have put animal fat, horsehair, wool, wire, wax, powder, plaster and even model ships in their hair? Sometimes their styles were so outrageously huge they could hardly walk or get through doorways. They even had to sleep sitting up so that they wouldn't ruin their hairdos! All this was in the name of hair-raising style. These days we have many terrific and much easier styles to choose from. In this book you'll see how to create french braids, twisted ponytails, coiled buns, cornrows and lots of other styles. You'll also learn how to add beads and ribbons to your hair, and how to make splashy scrunchees, one-of-a-kind barrettes and colorful hair bands. So get your brush, let down your hair and try some new styles.

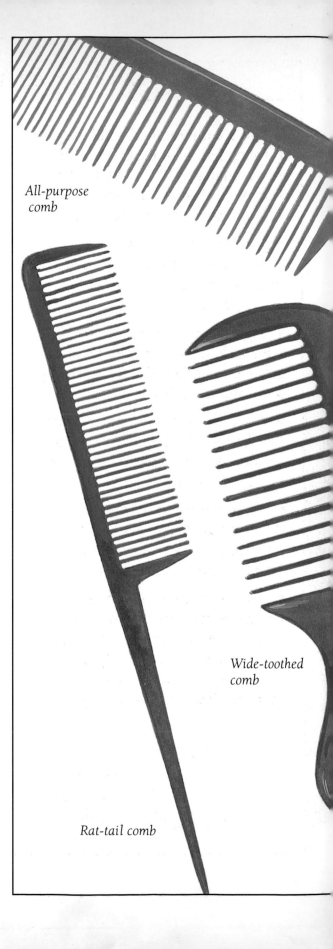

All-purpose comb

Wide-toothed comb

Rat-tail comb

HAIR TOOLS AND TIPS

• Use a wide-toothed comb to go through hair when it is wet or to remove tangles. To untangle hair, start at the bottom of a small section of hair and work your way up.

• A rat-tail comb is useful for parting hair, especially if you are making cornrows, which require many parts.

• A good all-purpose comb is one with wide teeth at one end and fine teeth at the other. Use it for parting and smoothing hair.

• A good quality all-purpose brush is a flat-back brush with synthetic bristles or a combination of natural and synthetic ones.

• A water mist bottle is handy to dampen hair. Water helps to get static out of hair and makes it easier to gather hair together.

• Covered hair elastics are much gentler on hair than rubber bands. They come in a few sizes and many colors. Keep lots on hand. You will need tiny rubber bands for cornrows and hair wrapping.

• Clips are good for holding some of the hair out of the way while you work on another section of hair.

• Bobby pins are fun to decorate and they're useful for holding hair in place.

• Hairpins are more open than bobby pins and they're especially good for holding buns in place.

• Decorated barrettes, scrunchees, hair bands and ponytail holders all add finishing touches to a hairstyle. To make them, you'll need plain barrettes, beads, fabric scraps, elastic cord and a few other items that you'll find around home or at a craft supply store.

Ponytail

Any type of hair, shoulder length or longer, will work nicely in a ponytail.

1 Brush the hair from the front and sides to the nape of the neck. Use the brush to gather the hair into your free hand.

2 Put down the brush and pick up a hair elastic while still holding the hair you have gathered. Stretch the elastic open between your fingers and thumb.

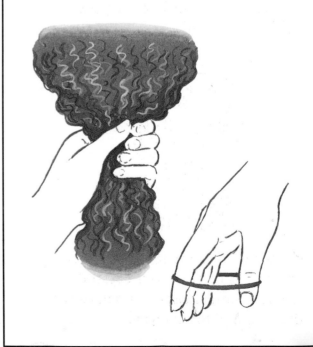

3 Grasp the hair with this hand, letting go with the other. Use your free hand to hold the elastic open as you pull the ponytail through it.

OTHER IDEAS

• Take a small section of hair from under the ponytail and wrap it around the elastic to cover it. Catch the end of this section of hair in a bobby pin and slide the pin through the elastic and out of sight.

• Instead of an elastic, use a ribbon, scrunchee, scarf or large barrette to hold the ponytail.

• If the hair is very long or uneven, try putting three or four colorful elastics, scrunchees or ribbons down the length of the ponytail.

4 Twist the elastic once and pull the ponytail through it again. Repeat until the elastic is tightly wound around the ponytail.

• To make a high ponytail, brush the hair upward from the nape of the neck and fasten it. Also try a side ponytail — the hair will need to be a little longer than shoulder length for this type of ponytail.

• If you want to make a very high ponytail, lie on your back on a bed and hang your head over the side. Brush and gather your hair on top of your head. You can use barrettes or bobby pins to hold stray hair or just let it hang down.

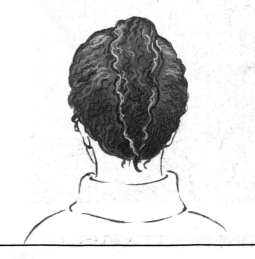

Half Ponytail

This quick style works well in hair shoulder length or longer.

1 Brush back the hair from above the ears and the top of the head into your free hand.

2 Fasten it in place with a hair elastic. (If the rest of the hair gets in the way, you may want to use bobby pins or clips to hold it down while you make the half ponytail.)

OTHER IDEAS

• If the hair is very long or thick, fasten it with a barrette or tie it into a knot. To do this, twist the hair and coil it into a doughnut shape. Pull the end of the half ponytail through the hole in the center.

French Ponytail

If your hair fits into a regular ponytail, it will fit into this style.

1 Brush back the hair from above the ears and the top of the head into your free hand. Use a hair elastic or mini-scrunchee to hold this hair in place.

2 Pull back more hair from behind the ears and gather it together with the hair already in the ponytail. Fasten it with another elastic.

3 Gather the rest of the loose hair and include it with all the other hair to make one thick ponytail. Fasten it.

Pull-back Styles

These styles work well with almost any length of hair, except very short hair.

1 Use the end of a comb to make a front or side part.

2 Comb or brush back the hair on each side of the head.

3 Fasten the hair in place with a barrette on each side of the head just above and behind the ears.

OTHER IDEAS

• If the hair is parted on the side, pull back and fasten only the fuller side.

• Try placing the barrettes in various positions, such as high above and behind the ears or in front of the ears close to the face.

• Use decorated bobby pins instead of barrettes. If the hair is heavy, cross a second bobby pin over the first one.

• Instead of holding the hair with barrettes, use ponytail holders to make mini-ponytails. If the hair is side-parted, you can make a ponytail on one or both sides.

• Try sweeping the side hair from above one ear over to the other side and hold it with a barrette or ponytail holder.

Inverted Ponytail

If you have a special tool for inverting a ponytail, you can use it. Otherwise, here's how to do it with your fingers.

1 Gather the hair into a ponytail. Pull the hair elastic a little away from the head.

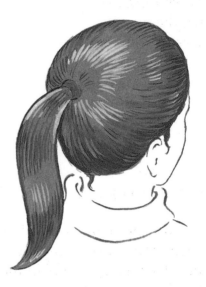

2 Poke your index finger and thumb up from the bottom into the center of the hair between the head and the elastic.

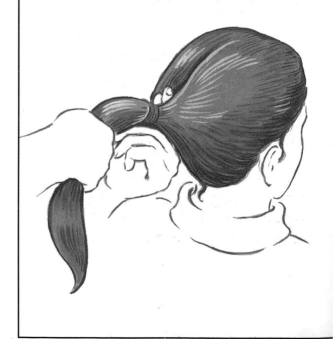

3 Lift up the ponytail with your free hand so that you can grasp it with your finger and thumb. Pull it down through the opening you have made.

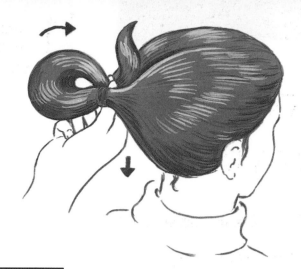

OTHER IDEAS

• If your hair is shoulder length but not much longer, make an inverted ponytail. Then take the end of the ponytail, lift it up as if you were going to invert it again, but this time just tuck the end of it down into the space close to the head. Secure the ponytail with bobby pins so it doesn't come loose. Make it fancy by tucking in fresh, dry or silk flowers.

• Hair can be as short as chin length for this style. Make a mini-ponytail on each side of the head (see page 11). Loosen the hair elastics. Poke your finger and thumb through the hair from underneath and flip each ponytail. For longer hair gather all the hair (including the hair from the mini-ponytails) into a high ponytail. Loosen the ponytail and invert it.

13

Basic Braiding

Hair must be longer than shoulder length to go in a full braid. There's more than one way to braid. These instructions will get you started and as you get better at it, you'll find a comfortable way to position your hands.

1 Brush the hair into a ponytail and fasten it with an elastic.

2 Divide the ponytail into three equal strands. Hold the left strand in your left hand and the right strand in your right hand. Let the center one hang loose.

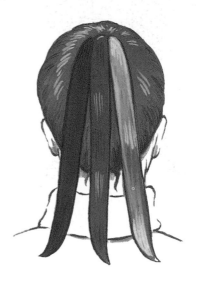

3 Pass the right strand over the center one and take it with your left hand.

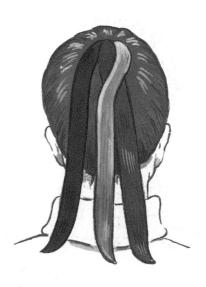

4 With your right hand, pull the original center strand to the right.

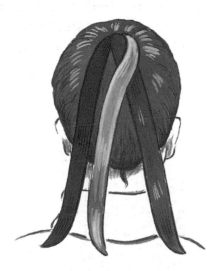

5 Pass the left strand over the center and take it with your right hand.

6 Continue by taking turns crossing the right strand, then the left, over the center until you run out of hair. Finish by wrapping a hair elastic around the end.

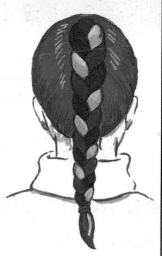

OTHER IDEAS

• Divide the ponytail into three or more sections and braid each one separately so you have many small braids.

• If the hair is straight, make one or more braids when it is damp. Sleep on the braids and undo them in the morning for wavy hair.

• Part the hair evenly, gather it into pigtails and braid them. These braids can be worn hanging down, coiled into mini-buns or crossed on top of the head and pinned in place for a "Heidi" look.

Ribbon Braid

Hair must be longer than shoulder length to go in a full ribbon braid.

1 Brush the hair into a ponytail and fasten it with an elastic.

2 Cut a length of ribbon twice as long as the ponytail plus 50 cm (20 in.). This will give you enough ribbon to tie a bow on the end. (If you don't want a bow, trim the ribbon.)

3 Tie the ribbon around the hair elastic and loosely knot it so that the ribbon ends are even.

4 Divide the ponytail into two even strands. Use the two ribbon tails together as the third strand and braid the ponytail.

5 Fasten the braid with an elastic. Separate the ribbon ends and tie them around the elastic to cover it.

OTHER IDEAS

• Try making a ribbon braid out of a half ponytail or pigtails, or make a small ribbon braid at the side of the head.

• If you already have a basic braid and would like to add a ribbon, simply tie a ribbon around the elastic at the top of the braid and criss-cross it down the length of the braid. Tie the ribbon ends around the elastic at the bottom.

Braided Hair Band

Hair should be shoulder length or longer for this style.

1 Use a comb to make a part from just behind one ear, over the head to the other ear.

2 Brush the front hair forward while you fasten the rest of the hair at the back.

3 Divide the front hair down the center. Braid each side just above the ear.

4 Cross the braids on top of the head and hold them in place with bobby pins. Tuck the ends under so they don't show. Release the back hair.

OTHER IDEAS

• Try pulling these side braids to the back, where they can be fastened together with a ponytail holder, scrunchee or barrette.

Basic French Braiding

All the hair (except the bangs if there are any) must fit into a high ponytail to work in a basic french braid. Don't worry if your first few braids aren't perfect. Keep trying and you'll soon get the hang of it!

1 Brush the hair to make sure it is smooth and tangle-free.

2 Take a section of hair from the crown of the head.

3 Divide this section into three strands. Begin braiding by crossing the right strand over the center and then crossing the left over the center. With your right hand, again cross the right strand over the center, and hold all three strands in your left hand.

4 With your right hand, gather a section of loose hair from the right side of the head. Add this hair to the strand of hair you just crossed over the center.

5 Use both hands to pull and make the braid tight.

6 Use your left hand to cross the left strand over the center. Gather a section of loose hair from the left side. Add it to the hair you just crossed over the center. Tighten the braid to the head.

7 Continue to braid, adding more hair each time you cross the center strand. Try to add the same amount of hair each time.

8 Basic braid the remaining hair. Fasten the braid with a hair elastic and finish with a scrunchee, ribbon or other hair holder.

OTHER IDEAS

• If you're trying to grow out bangs, start the french braid close to the forehead so the bangs can be worked into it.

• To make a french-braided half ponytail, braid only until you have included all the top and side hair. Take the strands you have in your hands and basic braid them to the end. Let this braid hang down with the rest of the loose hair at the back.

Side-to-Back French Braid

This style works best on hair that is shoulder length or longer. Once you know how to do a basic french braid, you'll be able to master this variation.

1 Part the hair down the center from the bangs to the nape of the neck.

2 Hold the right side of the hair in an elastic while you work on the left side.

3 Take a section of hair that goes from just in front of the ear to the center part and divide it into three equal strands.

4 Start braiding by crossing the left strand over the center, then the right one over the center.

5 Cross the left strand over the center again, adding hair from above the ear.

6 Cross the right strand over the center, adding hair from the center part.

7 Keep french braiding until you run out of hair to add. Basic braid about 5 cm (2 in.) farther and fasten with a hair elastic.

8 French braid the right side. Begin by separating the hair into three strands and this time cross the right strand over the center first, then the left strand.

9 Keep french braiding until you run out of hair to add. Then basic braid about 5 cm (2 in.) farther. Fasten hair with a covered elastic.

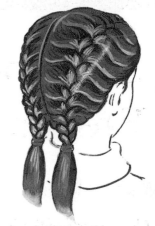

10 Gently pull out the elastics and combine the six strands to make three strands. Basic braid the rest of the hair. Fasten with an elastic.

OTHER IDEAS

• Coil the braid into a bun and fasten it with hairpins or a scrunchee.

• For french-braided pigtails, french braid one side until all the hair is included and basic braid the rest of the hair. Repeat for the other side.

• For a partial side-to-back braid, part the hair down the center or side. French braid each side to just beyond the ear. Basic braid the remainder and let the braids hang down with the loose hair at the back.

French-braided Hair Band

Hair doesn't need to be very long for this style — chin length or longer is fine.

1 Make a part from just behind one ear, over the head to the other ear. (If there are bangs, do not include them in the braid.)

2 To keep the rest of the hair out of the way while you braid, put it in a ponytail.

3 With the head tilted sideways, begin the french braid at one ear. Continue over the head and end the braid just behind the other ear.

4 Finish with a basic braid and fasten it with an elastic. Take the rest of the hair out of the ponytail.

Cornrows

Cornrows are like narrow french braids woven close to the head. If your hair has tight curls, it doesn't need to be very long for cornrows. If your hair is straight, it should be at least chin length. Try doing these with a friend.

1 Part the hair down the center from forehead to crown. If the hair is short, you may want to part it from the forehead to the nape of the neck. If there are bangs, you can either include them or begin the braids behind them.

2 Make another part 2.5 to 5 cm (1 to 2 in.) from the center. Take this section of hair from the forehead to the crown and fasten it with a hair elastic. You will braid this hair first.

3 Use clips, bobby pins or ponytail holders to fasten all the remaining hair so that it is out of the way. Take the hair to be braided out of the elastic.

Instructions continue on the next page ☞

4 Begin the braid close to the forehead. When you french braid such a narrow section of hair, add hair to each strand from *behind* the braid rather than from beside it.

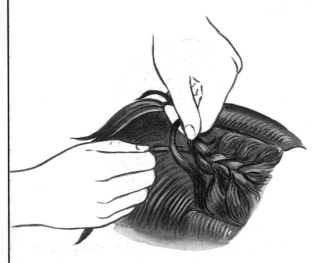

7 Continue making new sections and braiding until the hair is in cornrows across the front. You will likely find that having three to five rows on each side of the center part is enough.

5 Continue the cornrow to the crown (or to the nape of the neck) and then basic braid the strands to the end. Fasten the braid with a tiny, colorful rubber band.

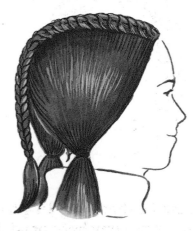

6 Unfasten some of the remaining hair so that you have a new section to braid into a cornrow.

8 You can leave the hair with the cornrow braids hanging down over the loose hair at the back or you can make small basic braids with the rest of the hair. To do this, part the hair in small, square sections. Braid each section, making sure the rest of the hair is out of the way.

9 To add beads, thread one onto the end of the braid and pull it over the rubber band. If you have trouble doing this, tie a 30-cm (12-in.) piece of strong thread into a loop. Thread a bead onto the loop. Poke the end of the braid into the loop and slide the bead off the thread and onto the hair.

10 Cornrows can be left in for a couple of weeks. Gently shampoo and rinse the hair without rubbing.

OTHER IDEAS

• Instead of making cornrows from front to back, try doing them from side to side.

• Instead of french braiding the cornrows to the head, make many basic braids all over. Start at the nape of the neck and section the hair into small squares. Fasten the rest of the hair with clips or bobby pins to keep it out of the way as you braid.

• Hair can be almost any length to have one or two tiny basic braids in it. Try putting one or two behind the ear, hanging down from a center or side part, in front of the ear or anywhere!

Fishtail Braid

Hair must be longer than shoulder length to be put in a full fishtail braid.

1 Brush the hair into a high ponytail and fasten it with a covered elastic.

2 Separate the hair into two equal sections. Hold the left one in the left hand.

3 With the right hand, take a pencil-size strand of hair out from the back of the right section of hair. Cross it over tightly to mix in with the left section.

4 Take hold of the right section of hair and place your right thumb so that it keeps the crossed-over strand of hair in place.

6 Take hold of the left section of hair and place your left thumb so that it keeps the newly crossed-over strand of hair in place. Let go with the right hand.

7 Keep repeating these steps until all the hair is in the fishtail braid. Fasten the end with a hair elastic.

5 Let go with the left hand and take a pencil-size strand of hair out from behind the left section. Cross it over the other crossed-over hair and mix it in with the right section of hair.

OTHER IDEAS

• The fishtail braid looks especially good when the crossed-over strands of hair are quite thin. Try pulling strands that are half a pencil-width out from behind each section of hair.

Twisted Ponytail

This style works best on hair that is long and not layered.

1 Gather the hair into a high ponytail and fasten it with a hair elastic. Divide it into two smooth, equal strands.

2 Begin by twisting the top part of the right-hand strand to the right.

3 Cross it over the other strand into your left hand, being sure to hold it tightly so it cannot untwist.

4 Twist the other strand (now the right-hand strand) to the right and cross it over the left strand. Keep twisting and crossing the strands this way.

5 Twist the strands to the end and fasten this ponytail with an elastic.

Coiled Bun

Hair should be a little longer than shoulder length for this style.

1 Brush the hair into a high ponytail and fasten it with a hair elastic.

2 Begin twisting the ponytail into a coil.

3 Tuck the end of the ponytail under the coils. Use hairpins to hold the bun in place. Be sure to catch hair from the bun as well as the hair under it. If the hair is not too thick, you can hold the bun in place with a scrunchee.

OTHER IDEAS

• Braid the ponytail before putting it into a bun.

• Make four or five small ponytails on the top of the head. Twist and coil each ponytail separately into a mini-bun. Fasten each with hairpins or bobby pins.

Hair Wrapping

If your hair is at least chin length, it will look good with one of these colorful, embroidery floss-wrapped sections. You may need to do this with a friend.

1 Take a very small section of hair from behind the ear, from the part in the hair, or from the temples. Use bobby pins, clips or a hair elastic to hold the rest of the hair out of the way.

2 Braid the section of hair. Tie it off with a tiny rubber band.

3 Choose three colors of embroidery floss. Cut each strand about 3 m (10 ft.) long. If your hair is very long, cut 4 m (13 ft.) of each. If it is chin length, cut 2 m (6½ ft.).

4 Hold the lengths of embroidery floss together. Make a slip knot so that one part of the floss is about 10 cm (4 in.) longer than the braid. The longer floss ends will be for wrapping.

5 Pull the braid through the loop of the slip knot and pull the knot tight as close to the head as possible.

6 Wind each of the three long ends of floss around your fingers to make a small bundle of floss. Fasten each with a tiny rubber band.

7 Hold out the braid along with the shorter strands and two of the floss bundles. Starting as close to the slip knot as you can, begin winding with one of the floss bundles. Pull floss out as you need it.

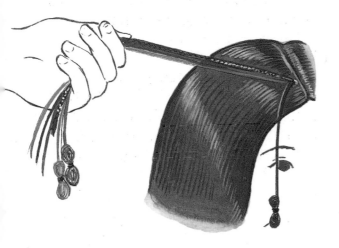

8 Wrap the braid with one color for about 2.5 cm (1 in.), then put it in with the other floss and the braid. Pick up another bundle and wrap with it, starting where the first color left off.

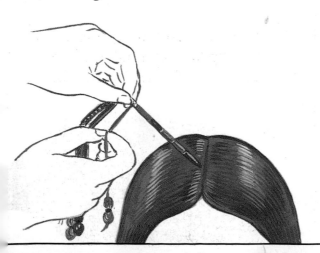

9 Continue wrapping and changing colors as often as you like. When you reach the rubber band on the braid, take it off and continue wrapping over the floss to about 2.5 cm (1 in.) past the end of the hair.

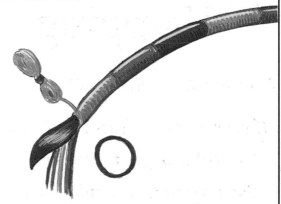

10 When you finish, knot the wrapping strand with one of the other strands. Then take all the six strands and tie them in an overhand knot. Trim off the ends.

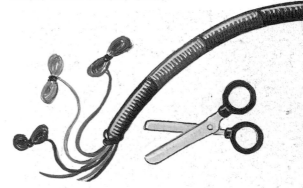

11 Your wrapped hair can be included in a ponytail or braid, tucked behind the ear or left hanging down. It can be washed with the rest of your hair, too. When you want to remove the wrapping, cut off the end knot. Unwind each color and cut the floss off as you go. Undo the tiny braid.

Scrunchee

A scrunchee can hold styles from a simple ponytail to a pretty coiled bun. Make them out of many different fabrics so you have some for everyday wear as well as for special occasions. Make a few extra scrunchees to give as gifts.

1 Cut or tear a piece of fabric 56 cm (22 in.) long and 10 cm (4 in.) wide.

2 Fold and pin it in half lengthwise with the good sides together.

3 Use the backstitch to hand stitch a seam along this pinned side (or sew it by machine). This seam should be about 1 cm (½ in.) in from the pinned side. Remove the pins as you sew.

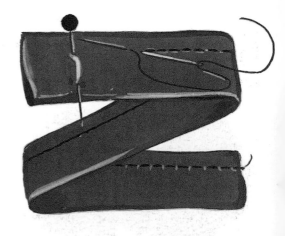

4 Fasten the safety pin to the seam area of one end. Tuck it into the fabric tube and weave it through to the other end to turn the fabric right side out.

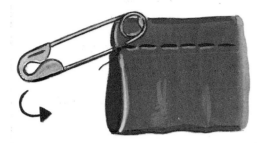

5 Cut a 23-cm (9-in.) length of elastic. Tape one end to your work table and fasten the safety pin to the other end. Thread the elastic through the tube using the pin.

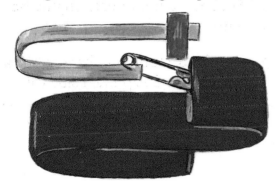

6 Remove the tape from the elastic. Overlap the ends of the elastic and sew them together.

7 Tuck one end of the tube into the other and try to match the seam. Fold under the unfinished edge of the fabric on top.

8 Stitch the folded edge to the tucked-in edge, all the way around.

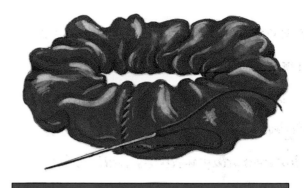

OTHER IDEAS

• You can make four mini-scrunchees out of the fabric needed for one regular scrunchee. Cut the fabric 28 cm (11 in.) long and 5 cm (2 in.) wide. Use a piece of elastic 15 cm (6 in.) long.

• Make a scrunchee hair band. Cut the fabric 64 cm (25 in.) long and 10 cm (4 in.) wide. Measure your head and use that measurement to cut the elastic — likely about 50 cm (20 in.) long.

Ponytail Holder

A ponytail holder can be worn to jazz up basic ponytails, half ponytails or braids.

YOU WILL NEED

strong round elastic cord

a ruler

scissors

2 large beads

1 Cut a piece of elastic about 30 cm (12 in.) long.

2 Thread both large beads onto it. Tie the elastic ends in an overhand knot.

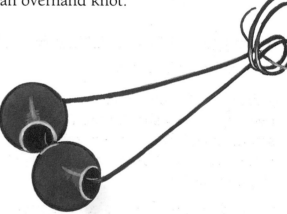

3 Pull the beads apart from each other. Position the knot in the center between them. (If the hole in one of your beads is large enough, tuck the knot inside it instead.)

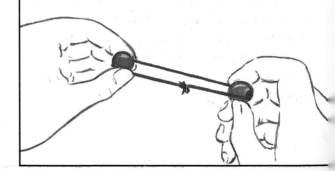

4 Pinch together the center areas of the elastic cord and tie a loose knot. Before you tighten it, make sure the knot is centered.

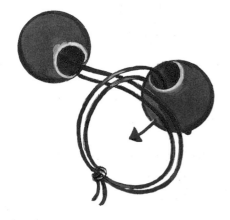

OTHER IDEAS

• Instead of using two large beads, use two large, fancy shank buttons or several smaller shank buttons. You can also make two special beads out of a modeling clay such as Fimo.

• Cut a length of elastic cord about 20 cm (8 in.) long. Thread on interesting shank buttons or beads until there is only enough elastic left to make a knot. Wrap this accessory around a ponytail.

• Cut a length of leather lace at least 50 cm (20 in.) long. Thread a few large-holed beads on one end. Knot the leather so that the beads can't fall off. Thread a few beads on the other end and knot it, too. Wear this hair accessory over a covered elastic on a ponytail. It can be loosely knotted.

5 To wear this ponytail holder, hold one bead on top of the ponytail as you wrap the other one around. Slide the wrap-around bead over the other one. If this isn't tight enough, wrap it around twice. Try to hide the knot.

Barrette

A barrette can be worn with almost any length or type of hair. It can be plain, fancy, large or small and as interesting as you can make it.

1 Measure and cut two rectangles of cardboard about 2 cm (¾ in.) longer than your barrette. They should be about 3 cm (1¼ in.) wide. Glue the rectangles together.

2 Cut a piece of fabric 3 to 4 cm (1¼ to 1½ in.) longer than your cardboard rectangles and twice as wide as them.

3 Place the fabric good side down and center the cardboard on it. Apply glue to the surface of the cardboard facing you.

4 Fold over the short sides of the fabric so they are held in place by the glue. You'll need to apply more glue to hold down the long sides. If you find the fabric is too bulky, trim off some of the edges. Allow the glue to dry for a few minutes.

5 Apply glue to the barrette. Place the barrette on the fabric-covered cardboard. Add more glue so that it overlaps the edges of the barrette and fabric. Allow it to dry for a few hours or overnight. (You may want to put rubber bands around the barrette to hold it together while the glue dries.)

BARRETTE BOW

Fold a piece of ribbon at least 20 cm (8 in.) long so that the ends overlap. Place it on a barrette. Slip another piece of ribbon the same length through the barrette. Tie it around the folded ribbon. Slide the knot under the barrette and glue the bow in place. Trim the ribbon ends and apply a thin coat of clear-drying glue or clear nail polish to the ends to keep them from fraying. Try using two or three different colors and widths of ribbon folded one on top of the other. Or use different colors and widths of ribbon to tie the bow.

BOBBY PINS

Plain bobby pins are fun to decorate, too. Slide on unique shank buttons, or glue tiny pearl beads, bows or small silk flowers onto them.

Hair Band

This is a great way to give an old hair band new life.

1 Measure the length of your hair band from one tip around to the other tip.

2 Cut or tear a piece of fabric that is 5 cm (2 in.) longer than the hair band. If the hair band is narrow, the width of the fabric should be about 5 cm (2 in.). If the hair band is a regular width, the fabric should be about 8 cm (3 in.) wide.

3 Pin the good sides of the fabric together along the entire length. Backstitch this length (or sew by machine).

4 Take a doubled piece of thread and tie it as tightly as you can around one short end to close it. Double knot the thread.

5 Use the knitting needle or pencil to turn the fabric right side out.

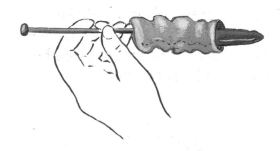

6 Push one end of the hair band into the open end of the fabric cover.

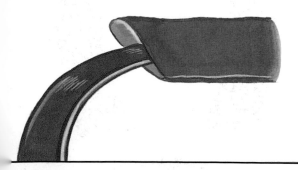

7 When the hair band reaches the closed end, arrange the fabric so that the seam is on the underside of the hair band.

8 Tuck in the edges of the fabric on the open end. Sew this end closed.

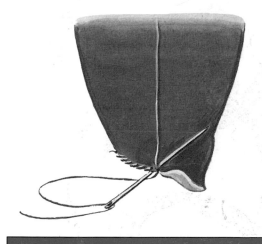

MORE HAIR BANDS

• Dress up a plain hair band by decorating it with fabric paint. Try criss-crossing narrow ribbon or flat lace from one tip to the other. Try tying, sewing or gluing on silk or dry flowers. You could also glue rhinestones or beads onto the hair band.

Special Occasions

Many of the styles in this book can be made to look extra fancy if you add fresh flowers to them or if you use accessories made from ribbons, lace, silk flowers or sparkly beads. Here are some other good ideas.

Long, straight hair

While french braiding, instead of keeping the braid close to the head, pull it out and away. Finish with a sparkly hair elastic. When you let it go, the hair drapes in tiers. Tuck in a few flowers and secure them with bobby pins.

Straight chin- to shoulder-length hair

Curl the hair with foam rollers, a curling iron or hot rollers. It's a good idea to apply some setting gel to the hair before curling it to help hold the curls. Pull back the hair at the sides and fasten it with fancy barrettes or use a hair band trimmed with fresh flowers to hold it back.

Curly or straight short hair

Use bobby pins with ribbons and pearl beads hanging from them to fasten flowers in the hair. Depending on how short the hair is, a decorated hair band or comb looks dressy, too.

Any type of hair, shoulder length or longer

If you're good at french braiding (or know someone who is!) try creating this braid: Start at one side of the face, go around the back of the head and up the other side. Basic braid the rest of the hair and coil it in a bun at the side of the head. Fasten it with hairpins and decorate with a flower.